Author's

This book features 100 influential and inspiring mindfulness quotes. Undoubtedly, this collection will give you a huge boost of inspiration.

1

"The first and best victory is to conquer self."

—

Plato

2

"For what it's worth, it's never too late to be whoever you want to be. I hope you live a life you're proud of, and if you find you're not, I hope you have the strength to start over."

—

F. Scott Fitzgerald

3

"We cannot become what we want by remaining what we are."

—

Max Depree

4

"Wherever you are, be there totally."

–

Eckhart Tolle

5

"Mindfulness gives you time. Time gives you choices. Choices, skillfully made, lead to freedom."

—

Bhante Henepola Gunaratana

6

"Nothing is worth more than this day. You cannot relive yesterday. Tomorrow is still beyond your reach."

—

Johann Wolfgang von Goethe

7

"You are the sky. Everything else is just the weather."

—

Pema Chodron

8

"Mindfulness isn't difficult. We just need to remember to do it."

–

Sharon Salzberg

9

"Everything is created twice. First in the mind and then in reality."

—

Robin Sharma

10

"Almost everything will work again if you unplug it for a few minutes. Including you."

—

Anne Lamott

11

"The only way to live is by accepting each minute as an unrepeatable miracle."

—

Tara Brach

12

"Nature does not hurry, yet everything is accomplished."

–

Lao Tzu

13

"Life is a dance. Mindfulness is witnessing that dance."

–

Amit Ray

14

"The two most powerful warriors are patience and time."

–

Leo Tolstoy

15

"How we pay attention to the present moment largely determines the character of our experience, and therefore, the quality of our lives."

—

Sam Harris

16

"Training your mind to be the present moment is the number one key to making healthier choices."

—

Susan Albers

17

"Within you, there is a stillness and a sanctuary to which you can retreat at any time and be yourself."

—

Hermann Hesse

18

"Mindfulness is deliberately paying full attention to what is happening around you— in your body, heart, and mind. Mindfulness is awareness without criticism or judgment."

—

Jan Chozen Bays

19

"Cultivating a generous spirit starts with mindfulness. Mindfulness, simply stated, means paying attention to what is happening; it's about what is really going on."

—

Nell Newman

20

"Realize deeply that the present moment is all you have."

–

Eckhart Tolle

21

"Meditation goes in. Prayer goes out. But both aim for the same place of union between you and the Divine."

—

Lisa Jones

22

"Mindfulness is a quality that's always there. It's an illusion that there's a meditation and post-meditation period, which I always find amusing, because you're either mindful or you're not."

—

Richard Gere

23

"Be where you are, not where you think you should be."

—

Unknown

24

"Sometimes the bad things that happen in our lives put us directly on the path to the best things that will ever happen to us."

—

Nicole Reed

25

"These mountains that you are carrying, you were only supposed to climb."

—

Najwa Zebian

26

"Mindfulness meditation should be more than just watching what you are doing. What you really need to watch is your motivation."

—

Thubten Zopa Rinpoche

27

"Worrying is stupid, it's like walking around with an umbrella waiting for it to rain."

—

Unknown

28

"No matter how difficult the past, you can always begin again today."

—

Jack Kornfield

29

"Feelings come and go like cloudys in a windy sky. Conscious breathing is my anchor."

—

Thich Nhat Hanh

30

"Be happy in the moment. That is enough."

–

Mother Teresa

31

"Mindfulness is a pause – the space between stimulus and response: that's where choice lies."

—

Tara Brach

32

"Each morning we are born again. What we do today is what matters most."

—

Buddha

33

"People have a hard time letting go of their suffering. Out of a fear of the unknown, they prefer suffering that is familiar."

—

Thich Nhat Hanh

34

"Mindul eating emphasizes a spirit of exploration, experimenting and flexibility in finding ways to make use of nutritional information."

—

Jean L. Kristeller

35

"Mindfulness meditation doesn't change life. Life remains as fragile and unpredictable as ever. Meditation changes the heart's capacity to accept life as it is."

—

Sylvia Boorstein

36

"Happiness, not in another place but this place... not for another hour, but this hour."

—

Walt Whitman

37

"Be where you are; otherwise you will miss your life."

-

Buddha

38

"Our life is shaped by our mind,
for we become what we think."

–

Buddha

39

"If you can't do anything about it, then let it go. Don't be a prisoner to things you can't change."

–

Buddha

40

"Quiet the mind, and the soul will speak."

–

Buddha

41

"Before you speak, let your words pass through three gates: Is it true? Is it necessary? Is it kind?"

–

Buddha

42

"You must not hate those who do wrong or harmful things, but with compassion, you must do what you can to stop them – for they are harming themselves, as well as those who suffer from their actions."

–

Buddha

43

"Rule your mind or it will rule you."

–

Buddha

44

"Three things cannot be long hidden: the sun, the moon, and the truth."

–

Buddha

45

"Just as a snake sheds its skin, we must shed our past over and over again."

–

Buddha

46

"When you move your focus
from competition to
contribution life becomes a
celebration. Never try to defeat
people, just win their hearts."

-

Buddha

47

"The desire to know your own soul will end all other desires."

–

Rumi

48

"Your heart knows the way.
Run in that direction."

–

Rumi

49

"As you start to walk on the
way, the way appears."

–

Rumi

50

"This universe is not outside of you. Look inside yourself: everything you want, you already are."

–

Rumi

51

"The body benefits from movement, and the mind benefits from stillness."

—

Sakyong Mipham

52

"Educating the mind without educating the heart is no education at all."

—

Aristotle

53

"When you focus on the good,
the good gets better."

–

Abraham Hicks

54

"In a world full of doing, doing, doing, it's important to take a moment to just breathe, to just be."

—

Unknown

55

"Your calm mind is the ultimate weapon against your challenges. So relax."

—

Bryant McGill

56

"In today's rush, we all think too much, seek too much, want too much– and forget the joy of just being."

–

Eckhart Tolle

57

"The mind is like water. When it's turbulent, it's difficult to see. When it's calm, everything becomes clear."

—

Prasad Mahes

58

"The mind is just like a muscle–
the more you exercise it, the
stronger it gets, and the more it
can expand."

—

Idowu Koyenikan

59

"Let go of the battle. Breathe quietly and let it be. Let your body relax and your heart soften."

—

Jack Kornfield

60

"Mindfulness means being awake. It means knowing what you're doing."

—

Jon Kabat Zinn

61

"The still waters of a lake reflect the beauty around it. When the mind is still, the beauty of the self is reflected."

—

Vanda Scaravelli

62

"Just when you feel you have no time to relax, know this is the moment you most need to relax."

—

Matt Haig

63

"When you want to succeed, as much as you want to breathe, then you'll be successful."

—

Eric Thomas

64

"The mind that opens to a new idea never returns to its original size."

—

Albert Einstein

65

"She was unstoppable, not because she did not have failures and doubts, but because she continued on despite them."

—

Beau Taplin

66

"Believe you can, and you're halfway there."

–

Theodore Roosevelt

67

"If you get tired, learn to rest
not to quit."

–

Banksy

68

"It always seems impossible until it's done."

–

Nelson Mandela

69

"Strong minds discuss ideas.
Average minds discuss events.
Weak minds discuss people."

—

Socrates

70

"When you replace 'why is this happening to me?' to 'what is this trying to teach me?' everything shifts."

—

Unknown

"He said, 'There are only two days in the year that nothing can be done. One is called yesterday and the other is called tomorrow, so today is the right day to love, believe, do, and mostly live."

-

Dalai Lama

72

"The ultimate source of my mental happiness is my peace of mind. Nothing can destroy this except my own anger."

–

Dalai Lama

73

"The true hero is one who conquers his own anger and hatred."

–

Dalai Lama

74

"If you think you're too small to make a difference... try sleeping with a mosquito in the room."

-

Dalai Lama

75

"Do not let the behavior of others destroy your inner peace."

–

Dalai Lama

"When you talk, you are repeating what you already know. But if you listen, you may learn something new."

-

Dalai Lama

"What is love? Love is the absence of judgement."

–

Dalai Lama

78

"In the practice of tolerance, one's enemy is the best teacher."

–

Dalai Lama

79

"The wound is the place where the light enters you."

-

Rumi

80

"Listen to silence. It has so much to say."

–

Rumi

81

"Live life as if everything is rigged in your favor."

–

Rumi

82

"Only the soul knows what love is."

–

Rumi

83

"Becoming awake involves seeing our confusion more clearly."

–

Rumi

84

"Just as water reflects the stars and the moon, the body reflects the mind and soul."

–

Rumi

85

"Our prime purpose in this life is to help others. And if you can't help them, at least don't hurt them."

–

Dalai Lama

86

"Remember that not getting what you want is sometimes a wonderful stroke of luck."

-

Dalai Lama

87

"The best way to take care of the future is to take care of the present moment."

–

Thich Nhat Hanh

88

"Yoga is the dance of every cell with the music of every breath that creates inner serenity and harmony."

–

Debashis Mridha

"Deep breaths are like little love notes to your body."

–

Unknown

"Yoga is a metaphor for life. You have to take it really slowly, you can't rush. You can't skip to the next position. You just have to breathe and let go."

—

Madonna

"When you practice yoga once a week, you change your mind. When you practice yoga twice a week, you change your body. When you practice yoga everyday, you change your life."

—

Unknown

92

"A small action done repeatedly can make an enormous difference."

—

Dr. Timothy McCall

93

"Every emotion is connected with the breath. If you change the breath, change the rhythm, you can change the emotion."

—

Sri Sri Ravi Shankar

"When the chest is opening, the mind is opening, and we feel emotionally shiny and stability comes."

—

Vanda Scaravelli

95

"You cannot breathe deeply and worry at the same time."

–

Sonia Choquette

"The body and mind are interdependent. They are inseparable in the art of introspection."

—

Geeta Iyengar

97

"Yoga does not change the way we see things. It transforms the person who sees."

–

B.K.S. Iyengar

"A mind is like a parachute. It doesn't work if it isn't open."

–

Frank Zappa

"If a cluttered desk is a sign of a cluttered mind, of what, then is an empty desk a sign?"

–

Albert Einstein

100

"Even if you're on the right track, you'll get run over if you just sit there."

—

Will Rogers

Printed in Great Britain
by Amazon

23449635R00056